FLANNEL JOHN'S EMERGENCY PREPARATION and BUG OUT BOOK

By Tim Murphy

For information on additional Flannel John titles visit www.flanneljohn.com

THERE IS NOT GOING TO BE A ZOMBIE APOCALYPSE, BUT...

The dead are not going to walk the earth and crave the taste of human flesh. It makes for interesting, even compelling, movies and television but it is not real. Disasters, natural and man-made, are real. Depending on where you live, your life may be impacted by a flood, tsunami, forest fire, tornado, hurricane, snowstorm, mud slide or power outage. In some cases, you may have to hunker down and ride it out. In other instances, you may have just moments to gather the family and bug out.

This book is meant to give you food for thought. If a disaster hits, what do you need to get you through the rough spots? What essential items should you have on hand to survive for a few days, a week or even a month? This book is not a comprehensive list, because everyone's situation is different. You probably won't need every item in this book. In fact, you won't need most of them. Some items may seem redundant, but it gives you options and in a pinch, barter. Consider these items as cheap insurance. It's better to have them on hand and never use them, rather than desperately need something you can't find.

HUNTING AND GATHERING

They are often called "Bug Out Bags." A gym bag, duffle, five-gallon bucket or tote stocked with your essential items in case of emergency. First, where should you keep it? You want quick access so options can be a closet by the front door, the trunk of car or in a camper. Watch out for extreme heat or cold. It can zap the batteries on portable items and mess with certain foodstuffs. If you live in a tornado area, consider storing the items in a 30-gallon trashcan in the basement with the lid secured.

When assembling your bag, don't over spend. Many of the items in this book you have sitting around the house in duplicate such as tools and blankets. You can scout thrift stores and garage sales. I have picked up transistor radios for as little as $2, sleeping bags for $4. A local thrift store had Freeplay wind-up radios and CBs for $5. You are not looking to spend high dollars to ascend Mt. Everest. The purpose is to have essentials on hand to grab in one spot. The bag I've put together cost me less than $150 and it was assembled over the course of a year. The most important points to remember: you need to stay warm, dry, fed, hydrated and safe. Keep that in mind while you hunt and gather these items that you hopefully will never need to use.

AIR MATTRESS & FOAM PAD

These will make sleeping so much more comfortable with your sleeping bags or blankets. Each one of these choices has advantages. Air mattresses can compress down to a small space but are not as durable. You also have to inflate them. Foam pads take up more space, are more expensive but are much more rugged.

ALUMINUM FOIL

Choose a heavy-duty version and take it off the roll. Fold it into a square. Use for cooking, storage and small repairs.

ALUMINUM OR METAL TAPE

Makes for strong, heat-resistant patching and repairs.

BATTERIES

Most devices use AA, AAA or 9-volt batteries. Larger flashlights rely on C or D cells.

BICYCLE

It is higher up the food chain of needs and necessities but depending on circumstances this can be a great mode of transportation if gasoline is scarce. A folding bike is small, portable, convenient and can fit in the trunk of a car or stow easily in a camper.

BINOCULARS

Remember those cheap, folding binoculars you had as a kid? Those will work. If you have access to a better model, grab it.

BLANKETS & SLEEPING BAGS

Warmth is a chief concern in emergencies. You can opt for blankets or sleeping bags. Your decision will depend on if you are sleeping in a camper, a car or outdoors. For emergency use consider a space blanket because it reflects heat back to your body.

BLEACH

Household chlorine bleach can be used as an effective disinfectant when diluted. Use traditional bleach. Do not use scented or color safe varieties or one with added cleaners. Mix nine parts of water with one part of bleach for disinfecting. In an emergency, it can be used to treat water for safety. Mix sixteen drops of bleach per one gallon of water.

BOOKS

Pack a book or two to keep you occupied and entertained. Don't forget a first aid manual.

BOOTS

You will want sturdy work boots, waterproof or water-resistant if possible. In the event of a disaster you don't know what kind of terrain or debris you will have to walk around, through and over. Protect your feet especially in the winter.

BUNGEE CORDS

These will help you hold it together...literally. Keep half a dozen of various sizes on hand.

CAN & CANDLE

Never underestimate the heat generated by a small candle in a tin can. Keep the candle short; making sure the flame does not get too high above the rim. Drill two holes near the top of the can and attach a piece of wire or coat hanger to act as a handle so you can hang the can like a lantern.

CAN OPENER

The stand-by P-38 can be found at army surplus and camping outfitters for under a buck. Although many brands of camping meals and freeze-dried food comes in foil or plastic pouches, canned food will always need an opener.

CB & HAM RADIOS

If the power is out and cell phone service unavailable, this is the best way to reach out and contact people and emergency personnel. Look for a battery operated walkie-talkie style CB radio. I found one at a thrift store for just $5. The antenna is built in and it can run independent of your vehicle. The other option is HAM radio. Though not the hobby it used to be, it is easier to get into today. You no longer have to take a Morse code test to get a license. In the event of emergencies, HAM Radio clubs often become the primary communication form in small rural areas. They also work in conjunction with other emergency municipal and county systems.

CELL PHONE BATTERY BACK-UP

There are several varieties of back-up batteries on the market that can extend your cell phone power. They use a USB plug and can fully charge a phone one to three times before they need charging themselves.

CLOCK

Small travel alarms can work for months on one or two batteries. A small wind-up alarm clock is also an option for ease and reliability.

CLOTHING

Be ready for all seasons in your area. It is function over form, don't worry about fashion. You want to focus on being warm, dry and protected. Keep these items in mind.

- Bandana
- Belts
- Carhart Outerwear
- Coats
- Hats
- Rain Gear
- Pants
- Socks, thick
- Shirts
- Sweatshirts
- Thermal/regular underwear

COAT HANGAR

There are times when a good solid piece of wire will come in handy.

COFFEE CAN WITH LID

Great for storage of small items and can be used to cook food in a pinch.

COLD WELD PUTTY

Think of it ask moldable duct tape. When things start to fall apart or break, it is a great item to have in your tool kit.

COMPASS

If cell phone service is not available, you won't have GPS capability. Direction will always be necessary information.

COOKING & EATING UTENSILS

Build your road kitchen...knives, forks, spoons, plates and my favorite, the spork. You will need a pot to boil water for making soup, coffee, tea and reconstituting freeze-dried foods. You can boil water over a fire or use a portable stove in a camp cup. For fuel use tinder, propane or Sterno. Mess kits and small aluminum pots and camp cookers can fill this niche.

COOKING FUEL OR STERNO

There are several varieties to choose from, Sterno probably being one of the most recognizable brands.

DISH SOAP

Aside from washing the kitchen gear, a tablespoon makes a very effective laundry detergent.

DOCUMENTS

Think insurance papers, titles, deeds, licenses, birth certificates, copies of ID cards, etc. You may not want to bring all of the original documents with you; a safety deposit box at a bank is best. Should you bring along photocopies or scanned copies on a thumb drive? Both. In the event of power outage or cell phone disruption, you may not have access to documents on a thumb drive or in the cloud so hard copies are important. Keep them in sealed plastic bags to prevent damage.

DRYER LINT

This fuzzy stuff you throw in the trash makes for an excellent fire starter. Mix with a little paraffin in a condiment cup or an egg carton and you are ready.

DUCT TAPE

It's been called a tool kit on a roll and it is. It works great for a quick patch of clothes, especially nylon coats. Make sure you get real duct tape, not a cheap, weak knock-off. Gorilla Tape also works quite well.

EMERGENCY TOOL

These 4-in-1 tools can be used as an emergency water and gas shut-off handle, a pry bar and a glass breaker. This is not needed in most situations but can be very useful under the right circumstances.

EYEGLASSES & REPAIR KIT

There is nothing worse than losing a screw and having the earpiece fall off. A few tiny screws and a small screwdriver can save a lot of frustration. Consider extra nose pads too!

FIRST AID KIT

Don't think small, think medium to large in size. It is better to have too many medical supplies than run short in an emergency. You can buy a ready-made kit or assemble your own. Here are some of the items to include:

- Absorbent Compress Dressings
- Adhesive Bandages (assorted sizes)
- Adhesive cloth tape
- Antibiotic ointment
- Antiseptic (bottle or wipes)
- Aspirin, Tylenol, Advil, etc.
- Cold Compress
- Hydrocortisone Ointment
- Non-latex gloves
  (latex allergies are common)
- Oral Thermometer
- Rolls of bandages
  (3 to 4-inch widths)
- Scissors
- Space blanket (Mylar)
- Sterile gauze pads (assorted sizes)
- Triangular bandages
- Tweezers
- First Aid Manual

FISHING TACKLE

A bottle cork or foam earplug can be used as a bobber. For size constraints, a collapsible pole and flies may do the trick depending on where you live and your fishing skills. You may laugh, but look for a Popeil Pocket Fisherman at a thrift store. They are cheap, effective and small. Some tackle to consider:

- Bobber
- Flies
- Hooks (store on a safety pin)
- Leader
- Line
- Lures
- Plastic worms
- Weights

FIVE GALLON BUCKETS

These can be purchased at hardware and home supply stores for cheap. Make sure you get a lid. You can use them to store most of your items for quick transport. They also protect food from bugs and moisture.

FLARES

Emergency road flares to attract attention and signal for help.

FLASHLIGHT

Choose a battery-powered or wind-up unit. A good heavy-duty Maglite is one of the best options. Plus in a pinch it makes an effective self-defense club.

FOOD

You want bang for your buck and your space. Think lightweight calorie dense foods. A five-gallon bucket can store enough edibles to feed four people for a week if you shop and pack smart. Here are some items to consider:

- Baby Formula/Baby Food
- Candy Bars
- C Rations
- Dried Food
- Dry Soup Mix
- Fast Food Condiment Packs
- Instant Coffee or Tea
- Granola Bars
- MREs
- Nuts
- Peanut butter and crackers
- Powdered Drink Mix
- Protein or Energy Bars
- Ramen Noodle Packages
- Spices
- Trail Mix

GAMES

Board games, cards games and dice can keep everyone entertained. If you are traveling with small children, consider paper, crayons and coloring books.

GAS CAN

A plastic, five-gallon gas can will give you what you need. It's small, light and depending on your vehicle it should get you 75 to 150 miles.

GLOVES

You need gloves, not mittens. Choose warm, rugged work gloves that are waterproof or water-resistant.

GROOMING & HYGIENE

You want to stay happy, healthy and clean.

- Antacids
- Baby Wipes
- Baby Powder
- Carmex or Lip Balm
- Comb or Hair Brush
- Contact Lens Solution
- Dental Floss (unflavored)
- Denture Adhesive
- Diapers
- Disposable Razor
- Feminine Products
- Hand Sanitizer
- Laxatives
- Nail Clippers
- Shampoo
- Shave Cream (or use soap)
- Soap (bar soap lasts longer)
- Toothbrush and toothpaste

HAND SAW

Choose either a foldable, fixed-handle or wire and ring model. The choice comes down to space and how much you think you will use it. This is necessary for clearing a campsite or cutting wood for a fire.

HATCHET

Good for firewood, clearing a camp site and personal protection.

ICE COOLER – ICE CHEST

The size depends on your needs, but I recommend a cooler that can hold ice for five days. This is not just for food, but certain medications need to be kept cold. Frozen jugs of water work great as an ice source and it also keeps the water clean for drinking as it melts.

IDENTIFICATION

Most people have a driver's license or some form of government-issued ID. You may want to consider a passport, military ID and Social Security card. You can also make photocopies for safekeeping and scan them on to a jump drive.

INSECT REPELLANT

Mosquitoes and flies can drive anyone insane. If you live near lakes or rivers you have put up with more than there fair share. If you are trying to survive a flood, the additional stagnant water is a breeding grown for mosquitoes. Netting is also an option to give you a good night's sleep.

LANTERN

Battery or solar-powered are the best choices. Lanterns are easier for reading and cast a wider light than a flashlight but not as far.

LIGHTER & MATCHES

You will need a fire source whether it's waterproof matches, flint or lighter. Disposable lighters are cheap and can do the trick. There is a trend back towards the old-style Zippos.

LOCKS

Keep the gear secured and the camper safe. If you brought a bike along, don't forget a lock for that too. I recommend a combination lock because keys can get lost.

MASON JAR CANDLE KIT

Put a piece of sandpaper on the exposed lid portion of a mason jar. Put matches and candles in the jar.

MAPS

Keep local, state and a road atlas on hand. Remember, GPS may not be working if cell phone service is down or interrupted.

MASK (DUST)

Not for Halloween but for breathing. If you're trying to get through a forest fire area or possibly a chemical spill these are indispensable. Think surgical masks like doctors wear.

METAL CAMP CUP

Use to boil water on portable stove or over a campfire.

METAL GRATE OR GRILL

Use a grate or piece of rigid metal mesh for cooking over a campfire. A 16-inch by 12-inch piece should do the trick.

METAL TIN FIRE STARTER

Mix cotton balls with petroleum jelly or wax in an Altoids tin or similar container. This makes for a perfect, portable fire starter.

MONEY/BARTER

Stash some small bills and coins as an emergency fund. It could be enough for a tank of gas or as much as you think necessary. In the event of difficult times, people may turn down money for food or water or even a source of fire. Pack a few items for barter because they will spend like cash under the right circumstances.

MULTI-TOOL, A LEATHERMAN OR A SWISS ARMY KNIFE

It's a tool kit in the palm of your hand. While a Swiss Army Knife has the versatility (some with dozens and dozens of options) they can sometimes get so big they become difficult to use. A multi-tool or Leatherman will have the ten or twelve tools you will really need.

NOTEBOOKS/PAPER

Keep yourself busy, doodle, write a journal, keep a log of the events and make notes.

PAPER TOWLS

Makes a great pillow until you need to clean up a mess.

PET CARE

Bring leashes, water bowl and dry dog food and vet records plus any medications they may need.

PHONE NUMBERS

Keep a hard-copy list of emergency phone numbers including family, friends, co-workers, government agencies, insurance companies, etc. You never know who you will need to contact in an emergency. If you store those numbers in a cell phone and the battery goes dead, you're out of luck.

PENS & PENCILS

You already have the paper, now you need a writing instrument. Grab a few pens and pencils. If you golf, check the bottom of your bag. I bet you'll find a dozen pencils mixed in with the tees.

PENCIL SHARPENER

You can use it to sharpen pencils, but it also works for shaving twigs and making tinder from the shavings. What an investment for 20 cents!

PLASTIC BOTTLES

Think small, a few ounces each. These bottles can keep lotions, shampoo, and detergent sealed and available. They can also store condiments.

PLASTIC GARBAGE BAGS

Aside from the obvious uses, bags can be used as makeshift rain ponchos or to black out windows in a car or camper for privacy.

POCKET HAMMOCK

If you find the right trees, it's a comfortable night's sleep.

PORTABLE SHOWER

Not an essential bug out item, but what a great feeling when you need one. There are two styles you can buy. The first is a thick, black, plastic bag with a spout. You put it in the sun and the bag absorbs heat, warming the water. They hold about five-gallons and are usually less than $10. I have seen these at thrift stores for as little as $2. The second style is a metal can with a built-in propane heater to warm the water. It's substantially more expensive and you will need a small propane bottle but you don't have to wait for a sunny day. It's a nice item to have for longer-term emergencies, but not really needed if you're displaced for a few days.

PORTABLE SOLAR GENERATOR

This is not a necessity for most people. It will depend on location and circumstances, but to have free power and the capability to recharge items from the sun cannot be underestimated. There are several manufacturers and models of these panels. If you're trying to get by for a few days, it's not really needed. If you are displaced for a week or more it can be invaluable, especially if the power is out and you're running low batteries.

PORTABLE STOVE

These are small, collapsible and are great to boil water for soup and to reconstitute freeze- dried foods. You will need fuel like Sterno for most models.

PRESCRIPTION MEDICATIONS

Because medications have an expiration date and refill limitations, you can't really stockpile for emergencies. Remember to bring those bottles along when you have to bug out as well as the name and numbers of your doctors who wrote those prescriptions.

RADIO

I have found transistor radios at thrift stores for $2. Sometimes old-school technology is the best. Consider a wind-up radio like the Free Play or solar powered units. Some wind-up models have a USB plug-in so you can charge your phone as you wind. A dedicated weather radio is also a wise purchase.

RAGS

For clean-ups, pillows or even as a fire-starter. Clean old t-shirts or towels are good choices.

RAIN PONCHO

You can buy disposable plastic ponchos for a couple of bucks or create a makeshift poncho from a large garbage bag. If you are in rainy or wet circumstance, you should opt for a more durable rain poncho at a cost of $5 to $10.

RAZOR BLADES or BOX CUTTER

A knife substitute making thinner cuts. A razor blade is also smaller and can be used as a defensive weapon.

ROPE OR PARACORD

Not just for tie-down and security, think laundry line. Thin paracord can also double as a strong fishing line or a snare.

SAFETY GOGGLES

Whether your cutting wood or repairing an engine, it's good to pack a pair.

SAFETY PINS

Use to make quick repairs, improvised fishing hooks or to hang a tarp for a makeshift shower stall/bathroom.

SCISSORS

You should keep a small pair in the first aid kit or sewing kit. Keep a larger, heavy-duty pair on hand for tougher or more intricate cuts.

SELF DEFENSE

In times of emergency, helping someone is at the top of most people's thoughts. Unfortunately, opportunists can take advantage of dire situations so you do need a form of protection. Guns, rifles, shotguns, knives, hatchets, tasers, mace or pepper spray are all a matter of personal preference and in some circumstances, state law. Always check your state's regulations when it comes to these items if you are unsure. If you do opt for a firearm, don't forget ammunition and CO_2 cartridges for air pistols.

SEWING KIT

Keep it together by keeping your clothes together. A sewing kit can also serve as a makeshift suture kit in a medical emergency. You should have:

- Needles (several sizes)
- Needle Threader
- Thread (several thicknesses)
- Thimble
- Scissors

SHOE & BOOT LACES

They always seem to break at the worst moment so have back-ups.

SHOVEL

A small shovel or a folding shovel can be a big help around the campsite or in snowstorms and winter emergencies.

SIGNAL FLAG

A safety orange or red flag can be a call for help. Keep this in your vehicle. If you get into trouble or are stuck because of a snowstorm, tie it to your car's antenna. An upside down American flag is also an emergency signal.

SIGNAL MIRROR

Used more for stranded parties in remote locations but if you need to get attention from a distance it works.

SLING SHOT

For hunting and self-defense it's old school but effective. Use pellets, ball bearings or rocks for ammunition. It works in hunting small game and unlike a gun it's quiet and doesn't draw attention.

SUNSCREEN

Look for an SPF 30 or better. Remember, you are not looking for a tan you are looking for protection.

SUNGLASSES

Eye protection and sun protection are not only for your health but to prevent fatigue.

SUPERGLUE – GORILLA GLUE

If duct tape or cold weld putty doesn't work, it's time to use these.

SURVIVAL KNIFE

Invest in a good quality, strong, sharp knife. This is one of the few things you should not buy cheap. This will have so many useful applications. Invest in a good protective sheath and sharpener too.

TARPS OR PLASTIC SHEETING

Whether as a makeshift tent, ground cover for sleeping bags, poncho or suspended for a shower a good tarp is worth its weight in gold.

THUMB DRIVE - JUMP DRIVE (USB)

Thumb drive or jump drive, whatever you call it, is a true must carry item. Scan copies of all of your important documents, insurance papers, titles, birth certificates, etc. Even if electricity is out, you will eventually be able to access the papers. Scan important family photos on to it as well.

TIRE CHAINS - TIRE CABLES

These are not legal in all states. Strap them on your tires to get you through snow and out of bad situations. Don't put them in the bug out bag; keep them in the trunk of your car.

TOILET PAPER

I can't emphasize how important and how easy this will make your life! Extra paper also makes for great bartering. Purchase single, individually wrapped rolls.

TOOLS

Build a tool kit: hammer, rubber mallet, wrench, pliers, file, screws, nails, bolts, etc.

TOW STRAPS

A passerby is more likely to help you out when you have the proper tools on hand.

TOWELS

As we learned in the "Hitchhiker's Guide to the Galaxy," a towel is an essential item when traveling.

VITAMINS

Stress can wreak havoc on health. Vitamins can keep you balanced especially if you are not eating consistently.

WALKIE-TALKIES

If cell service is down, you will be able to communicate with family and friends if you have a pair. Communication can be a lifesaver.

WALKING STICK/STAFF

This is not just for sure footing but excellent as a self-defense weapon.

WATER & WATER BOTTLES

Collapsible five-gallon water containers with a spout are readily available at camping and outfitter stores. Fill it from the tap before you hit the road if you have time. Dollar stores around the country sell six-packs of water. Emergency water in cans or pouches has a longer shelf life. Your choice will depend on location and the types of emergencies you anticipate in your area. Because of the weight, large amounts of water can be difficult to transport. Grab enough for an immediate need, a couple of days.

WATER PURIFIER OR TABLETS

Water sources can be questionable after disasters. Purifying tablets and small purifiers can save you from sickness and even death. Read the instructions on both and use appropriately.

WD-40 OR LIQUID WRENCH

It's a toolbox in a can.

WHISTLE

Signal for help or alert others of your location.

WINE CORK

Makes a great inexpensive and durable fishing bobber. If you live near water, attach a cork to your sunglass lanyard or keys to keep them afloat. They can also be used to hold needles and pins for a sewing kit.

ZIP LOCK BAGS

Use them to mix or store food and to keep documents and valuables dry.

ZIP TIES

They are cheap, strong and available in several sizes and lengths. Grab a handful and throw them in your bag.

If you are looking for more books from author Tim Murphy, including his "Cookbooks for Guys" series visit www.flanneljohn.com.

FLANNEL JOHN'S
HUNTING & FISHING CAMP
COOKBOOK
"A Good Meal Always Makes for a
Good Day"

FLANNEL JOHN'S
WOODS & WATER COOKBOOK
"Critters, Fritters, Chili & Beer"

FLANNEL JOHN'S
PIRATE GALLEY COOKBOOK
"Coastal Cuisine and Maritime Meals from
Oceans, Lakes & Rivers"

FLANNEL JOHN'S
MOUNTAIN MAN COOKBOOK
"Frontier Food from the Hills, Country
and Backwoods"

**FLANNEL JOHN'S
TAILGATING GRUB & COUCH POTATO
COOKBOOK
"Food for the Football Fanatic"**

**FLANNEL JOHN'S
SINGLE GUY COOKBOOK
"Simple Recipes with
Six Ingredients or Less"**

**FLANNEL JOHN'S
HEARTY BOWL COOKBOOK
"Soup, Stew, Chili & Chowder"**

**FLANNEL JOHN'S
HUNTING CABIN COOKBOOK
"Venison, Fowl & Wild Game"**

**FLANNEL JOHN'S
FISHING SHACK COOKBOOK
"Fish, Shrimp, Clams,
Crabs and Oysters"**

FLANNEL JOHN'S
COOKBOOK FOR GUYS
"Anthology – Volume 1"

FLANNEL JOHN'S
CAR GUY COOKBOOK
"Food for the Gastronomic Gearhead"

THE TUBE STEAK BOOGIE COOKBOOK
"A Celebration of Hot Dogs, Brats,
Sausage & Kielbasa"

THE ROCK AND ROLL COOKBOOK
"You Cook Me All Night Long"

THE KILLER BURGER COOKBOOK
"When You're Mouth Is Full, No One Can Hear
You Scream"